My Search

Josef Ben-Eliezer

The Plough Publishing House

Published by The Plough Publishing House of
The Bruderhof Foundation, Inc., Rifton NY 12471 USA
and by Bruderhof Communities in the UK
Robertsbridge, E. Sussex, TN32 5DR UK

ISBN 0-87486-932-3

Printed in the UK

IN THIS GREAT CONFUSION there are innocent people with pure hearts who are at a loss, shaken by what they see, who ask with pain and sorrow: "Where will our help come from? Who will guide us and give us an example through their life, by their behaviour? Who can we follow?" Young and old search for true light with deep longing, wrestling with their doubts.

Natan Hofshi, Israeli pacifist (1889-1980)

Contents

Grandmother, Lena, Judith, Mother, Uncle Milech, Josef, Leo

1. Earliest Memories

I WAS BORN IN JULY 1929, in Frankfurt, Germany. My parents were Eastern European Jews who had come several years earlier from Poland. Unlike the Jews who had lived for generations in Germany, they knew little or nothing about German culture, like Goethe and Schiller. The German Jews were wealthier, better educated and patriotic; they considered themselves a real part of German society. But we did not feel so much at home there.

At the time of my birth, my brother Leo was already eleven and my sister Lena ten. So for a year and a half, I was the baby in the family. Then even after my younger sister, Judith, was born, I received a lot of attention because I was often sick. My parents had established a fairly comfortable living by then, so I was pretty spoilt as a child. We shared a house with several relatives from my mother's family and I used to play with my cousins.

My parents had a kind of warehouse together with my Uncle Chaim Simcha. In Germany, young women often used the income from their first job to buy an *Aussteuer*, a set of sheets, pillows and blankets – maybe even a featherbed – for the time when they would marry. My father and uncle sold such sets of linens to be paid off in monthly instalments. The business went well and I think my extended family acquired several properties in Frankfurt. So we were fortunate that we had the means to escape Germany when the Nazis came to power.

My memories of Frankfurt are varied and scattered: an exciting visit to the Frankfurt Zoo, dreadful throat examinations in kindergarten, a fantastic candy shop around the corner from our house.

My first memory of anti-Semitism was my mother's horror when I came home and used the expression *Dreckjude* ('filthy Jew'). As a three-year-old, I must have picked it up from playmates without understanding what it meant. Later we watched from the windows of our house as the SA marched through the street singing, 'When the Jewish blood will run from our knives…' More than my own fear, I remember the look of terror in my parents' eyes.

When Hitler came to power in January 1933, my parents were convinced that we needed to leave Germany.

In April, Father went to Palestine to find a home for us there. We waited anxiously for news; eight months we waited. But in the end he could not secure permission from the British authorities for us to enter Palestine. He sent word that we should meet him in Poland, because he felt it was unsafe for him to return to Germany. After a joyful reunion at the train station in Rzeshov, we made our way to my mother's hometown of Rozwadów where we were to spend the next six years.

Leo and friend,
Josef and friend
outside their house
in Rozwadow

2. Rozwadów – Life in the Stetl

ROZWADÓW WAS A SMALL TOWN, maybe around five thousand people. In the middle of town was a square – huge in my memory – where a market was held once a week. A busy road went right through the square. Very occasionally we saw a motorcar go through, but there was always bustling traffic of horses and wagons. My good friend was a man who delivered goods for my father. He had fled from communism in his native Georgia and was quite poor. I loved to spend time with him and with his family. It was fascinating to watch him as he made ropes. He also told wonderful stories in his unique Yiddish dialect.

We lived in a terraced house along one side of the square. At the back of the house was a yard stretching one to two hundred metres out to a dirt road. We shared a well with our neighbour. A wood stove heated the house. There was no running water and we had an outside toilet. It all sounds quite primitive now, but at the time it was normal; everyone lived like that.

My father ran a wholesale business in sugar and other commodities. He bought in big quantities and supplied shops in a large area around Rozwadów. The goods were stored in the ground floor and cellar rooms of our house. We lived in the upstairs rooms. I often listened to him discussing business with my mother. They didn't think I understood it, but I was very curious about the business and I took it all in. The problem was always cash flow. People bought things on credit and then couldn't pay. It was a constant worry for my parents.

Occasionally, my father also had stores of candy. At such times I was frequently in the shop at the front of the house asking for some. At other times, I was also often in the shop – mostly begging for money to buy candy at the shop down the road. I was a finicky eater and my parents would sometimes pay me for eating my meals. Father was fairly strict with money, but after Alte Chaiya, my grandmother, came to live with us, I usually got what I wanted. She had first stayed on in Germany, but as we began to hear more and more about what was happening in Germany, my mother finally convinced her to come and live with us.

Alte Chaiya's death was a real blow to our family, although she was well over eighty. She was frying eggs one morning for Leo's breakfast. Suddenly she called our mother over and told her it was time for her to go. Mother couldn't believe she was serious; she hadn't been sick or anything. But Alte Chaiya simply lay down on her bed and peacefully passed away.

Rozwadów was probably half Jewish and half Catholic and we lived in a mixed neighbourhood. The butcher's shop two or three houses away from us usually had pork hanging in the window. One of our close neighbours was Polish. But we had very little contact with them.

There was a strong feeling of community among the Jewish people, in spite of all the differences between rich and poor, in spite of gossip, intrigue and all kinds of things. Jews did not have full rights in Poland, but we were not restricted in our contacts with Poles. I'm sure my parents dealt often with Poles in their business, but as a child I didn't have any contact. In fact, I only learned Polish when I started school. We avoided the Catholic Church, where we heard that they worshipped idols. And we were always afraid of the Christians, especially at Easter. After their church service, they would often go out on pogroms, trying to break into the shops. So at Easter time, or any of the Christian holidays, we would lock up our shops.

Very soon after we arrived in Rozwadów, my father said to me, 'Well, Josef, you have to go to Chaider'. This was the traditional Hebrew school for Jewish boys. There we learned Hebrew, starting with the alphabet. The melamet, or teacher, led us in chanting the letters together in a sing-song voice and he was not afraid to use the stick to keep order. Later, we learned parts of the Pentateuch by repeating after him. We must have learned something there, because I picked up Hebrew quickly when I later arrived in Israel.

We boys were quite a handful for our teacher. The boys had found out that if they formed a line and one touched the live wire in the circuit box, the last boy in the line felt the shock. So that shock was my rude introduction to Chaider as a four-year-old. If the teacher left the room, bedlam broke out among the fifteen to twenty boys. Even if he was there, some risked beatings to play cards under the table. I remember one older boy who collected money from the other boys – selling each one a tree in Palestine. I never saw my tree, but I certainly learned a few business tricks from him.

When I was seven, I had to go to Polish School, so my parents and my brother and sister taught me to answer a few simple questions: what my name was, where I was born, the name of my father and mother and that kind of thing. In time, I learned the basics of the Polish language and I was quite good in math, but I have no happy memories of that school. Quite apart from the language difficulties, the Polish children, and even the teacher looked down on the Jewish children and generally made our lives miserable.

We didn't often gather as a family for a meal. Mother or Lena would just run up from the shop and cook something for the children. In the evenings, it was a little more gathered. On Sundays, we had to close the shop, so we often went on excursions. Businessmen would go to the river. On Saturdays Jewish people did no business and we did not walk long distances, but on Sundays and general holidays we took the chance to do this kind of thing. I remember happy family excursions by the River San, also having picnics.

I was quite a nervous child with many health problems and I didn't eat properly. I often went to the dentist – probably because of my incorrigible sweet tooth. When I was about five, I had some kind of growth on my toe. Someone told my mother about a man who could help; I don't think he was a proper doctor. He put some powder on the growth and I let out a blood-curdling scream that still rings in my ears. The growth never came back, but I've had a scar from that treatment ever since.

Once I had to spend several weeks in Kraków where a

specialist treated my infected ear. I have terrible memories of how he scraped the pus out of my ear each day. But when we came home, my parents bought me a tricycle. This was quite a novelty in Rozwadów.

When I was about nine, my mother took Judith and me to the Carpathian Mountains for several weeks' holiday. I still have a photo of us standing with a man in a bear costume hugging us. I think this was also an effort to improve my health.

We had not actually planned to stay in Rozwadów. My parents still wanted to go to Palestine. Uncle Chaim Simcha and his two boys were already there. I guess they had slipped through before the British tried to stop the influx of German refugees. Father often told exciting stories about what he experienced in the eight months that he was there. He made it sound very interesting and glamorous, so I dreamed of one day going to Palestine, the Promised Land.

Sprinze, Mother, Milech,
Grandmother, Rahel

3. Religious life

CELEBRATION OF THE SHABBAT formed the centre of our religious tradition. Friday afternoon, Father took me to the *mikveh*, or ritual baths. First, each one poured a bucket of water over himself and washed with soap. Then we went into a kind of sauna, a steam-filled room with about twenty long steps going up one side. I managed to climb to the fourth step, but the higher steps were too hot for me. After this, we immersed ourselves in cold water. We emerged from the *mikveh* clean – inwardly and outwardly. Then we dressed in our best clothes and returned home for the lighting of the Shabbat candles. This ceremony moved us deeply and Mother often had tears in her eyes as she lit the candles.

After the candles were lit, Father, Leo and I went to the synagogue for evening prayers. The ancient melodies sung by the *Vorbeter* pierced my heart. I could understand only a few of the Hebrew words, but the melodies and the feeling of those chanted prayers expressed clearly the persecution and suffering of our people, the longing for God and for redemption. I re-live those Friday evenings still today when I secret myself away and listen to my scratchy recordings of Yossele Rosenblatt.

If any traveller or stranger was at the synagogue, it was considered a mitzvah, a good deed, to bring him home for the Shabbat meal. Mother always hoped that Father would bring someone along and he often did. Father led us into the house singing, 'Peace Be Unto You from the Watching Angels' and, 'Who can find a virtuous woman? For her price is far above rubies.' We washed our hands ceremonially and gathered around the festive table. He blessed the wine and then the *Challah*. The meal then went on for hours: maybe *Gefielte Fisch* followed by *Lokchen mit Yoch* and then a dessert. After the meal, Father read to us from Sholom Aleichem or from other famous Yiddish authors. To close the long evening, we sang many prayers and psalms together.

Sabbath morning we slept in. After a light breakfast – maybe coffee cake – the whole family went to the synagogue. Friday evening was solemn, but on Saturday morning there was a more social atmosphere. I loved to watch the reader open the special cupboard where the scrolls of the Torah were stored, pointing towards Jerusalem. He removed the velvet covering in the prescribed way and laid them out on the pulpit in the middle of the synagogue. My father or other men from the congregation were called up to the special honour of assisting the reader.

There were many rituals associated with the readings from the Torah and the prophets. These were solemnly performed, but a casual, untroubled atmosphere tempered the meetings. During the long readings, my father sometimes nodded off; another man might then come up behind him, pull on his ears and then pretend that he had done nothing. The meetings went on for hours.

During such meetings, my mother was in the women's part of the synagogue. I think they took it all more seriously than the men. Even though she didn't understand Hebrew, you could see that she felt it in her heart. The younger children could go freely between the men's and the women's sections; often I found my mother weeping.

After a substantial meal, we usually settled down for an afternoon's nap. Sometimes, my father took me with him to the rabbi's house. In some ways, this was the focus of spiritual life for the men. They discussed Scripture and the Talmud with the rabbi. My brother Leo didn't come with us; he was busy with his activities in the Zionist Youth Movement.

When the first stars appeared in the evening, we went again to the synagogue. But the real closing ceremony was held at home. We had another meal and sang praise to God who made the difference between light and darkness, between holy and secular. We followed Shabbat – "the queen" – to the door and bid her farewell for another week. Then business started again; we had to think about tomorrow.

4. Refugees

I WAS TEN YEARS OLD when the war broke out. It broke like a thunderbolt into a sunny summer day. The culture, religious and ethnic life of Rozwadów was shattered forever. People were glued to their radios. We soon realized that the invading Germans were advancing rapidly through Poland, and the Polish army was defeated. Masses of Polish soldiers started retreating through town – among them many Jews. Mother and a few other women set up an outside kitchen to cook food for the soldiers.

My father's business was destroyed long before the Germans arrived. First, Polish army officers came and requisitioned most of the sugar and rice. They gave us receipts, but even at the time we had no hope of ever receiving any payment. Afterwards, chaos and riots broke out. Mobs of Polish people wandered the streets breaking into shops and looting. They stole everything that was left in our shop.

We feared that the Germans would send the able-bodied men to forced labour camps, so my father and twenty one-year-old brother fled towards the Russian border. They returned home after about two weeks, however, because the German armies had already moved ahead and closed the border.

When the Germans moved in on Rozwadów, they took the town in a matter of hours. We spent the night in the cellar listening to the sound of explosions and artillery fire. Afterwards, my father and brother hid in the attic and we were to tell the Germans that they had left for Russia.

As a ten year old I didn't understand all the immense happenings. We ran around in the town, looking at the soldiers. I remember once standing in the square and watching a German officer gather his troops for a pep talk. He walked up and down in front of the soldiers who were standing at attention. Since German is so close to Yiddish, I understood some of it: 'Well, men! We have conquered here, and we've conquered there. We have planted seeds into all these different countries. Germany is going to take over the world.'

We were not allowed to meet in the synagogue, or have any gatherings. But since it was *Yom Kippur*, we gathered in one of the houses where we conducted the prayer. I can never forget this ardent crying out to God for his intervention and protection. No one knew what was ahead of us, but everyone expected the worst.

About a month after the Germans arrived, all Jews were ordered to gather in the square within an hour. No one said what was to happen, but we packed all we could carry on our backs. German officers – SS as I now suppose –

ordered us to march towards the River San. They shouted and drove forward these long lines of men, women and children, all carrying as much as they could manage. One drove by on a motorbike harassing everyone to go faster. He struck my father down with his bayonet. I don't think my father was badly hurt, but the experience made a deep impression on me.

When we finally arrived at the River San, there were more soldiers. I can't remember how we crossed the river, but I remember the soldiers searching us and taking any valuables. As so often, my father had foreseen what might happen and had sewn our money into my younger sister's underclothing. Many people were left with nothing, but we thankfully managed to cross over with some money as well as fur coats and other valuables.

The eastern bank of the San was a kind of no-man's-land. Apparently, Hitler and Stalin were still arguing over who would take it. We managed to find some temporary lodging in a village there. But it was unclear whether that area would be under the control of the Germans or the Russians, so no one wanted to stay there for long. My father and some other families managed to buy a horse and wagon so that we could move on towards the Russian-occupied area.

Not long afterwards, we heard that the Germans were advancing, so we loaded all our goods and some of the younger children onto the wagon and headed east. As we passed through a forest, some robbers appeared from nowhere with pistols, and ordered us to stop. We were all frightened, of course, but one courageous man stood up and said, 'You can kill me if you like, but we will fight for this wagon.' One of his sons stood by him and picked up a stone. The robbers grabbed a bike from the cart, but then they went away and let us pass.

As night fell, it was too dangerous to continue, so we retraced our steps a few kilometres to a Jewish inn. Many Jews were staying there. Late in the night, villagers came and surrounded the inn shouting abuse at us and taking the wheels off our wagons. We were completely surrounded and I was convinced that these Poles would kill us all. But suddenly, one of the Polish men jumped up onto a wagon and shouted at his fellows. 'Aren't you ashamed of yourselves for attacking such helpless people? Tomorrow it will be you. Everyone go home! I am standing here with my son, and if anyone touches these people, it will be over our dead bodies.' This stopped the mob in its tracks and the people slowly dispersed. I have never heard anything of this man before or after that night, but I will always have the greatest admiration and respect for his virtue and courage to speak out against that angry mob.

After about a week, we managed to reach Russian-occupied territory. The distance was not great, but it was slow going. We travelled by day through the forests and rested at night in the villages. The advancing Germans actually overtook us during that week, but they didn't hinder us.

We all rejoiced to see the Russian soldiers at last and know that we had escaped the Germans. That place –

called Lanzit, I think – was overflowing with refugees, so we squeezed into a train to Lvov hoping to find lodging there. Lvov was also crowded, but we had a distant relative, a merchant who let us stay in one of his storerooms.

We were grateful to have a roof over our heads, but our winter 'home' in Lvov was not a happy one. The storeroom must have been about five metres wide and about fifteen metres long. We shared the room with my Uncle Milech and his wife Rahel; but our two families often quarrelled. That storeroom was dim and cold. I can't remember any fire, but we may have had a wood stove – also for cooking. I don't remember going to synagogue in Lvov; in fact, I can't remember any religious life there at all. I suspect we were all more concerned with survival during those six months.

Our euphoria on first meeting the Russians faded quickly as we saw what life in Russia was like. My sister and I started to go to school during that time. The teacher held classes in Yiddish, but he was a communist and he tried to indoctrinate us into the personality cult that surrounded Stalin. I remember one song: 'There will always be streams running in the world, there will always be stars in heaven, but Stalin's name will shine over all of that, his name is deeper than the seas and higher than the mountains. There is nothing like him to be found in all of the earth.' Even we children felt this was ridiculous; we even argued with the teacher asking, 'Who then created the world?' But we also had to be careful; people suffered exile to Siberia – if not worse – for opposing Stalin.

To make some kind of living, we started dealing on the black market. By watching the shops and standing in long queues, we could sometimes get hold of cigarettes, sweets, and other rare commodities. Even I was sent off sometimes to sell things on the market, especially sweets. I wandered the streets during those months. If I wasn't selling things from a tray, I was mostly jumping trams and doing other stupid things that seem adventurous to a ten-year-old boy. It's a wonder that I wasn't killed.

In June 1940, the Russians issued a decree requiring refugees and other non-residents of the Ukraine to register with the police. We were given a choice. If we wanted to stay, they would grant us Soviet citizenship and help us resettle in the interior of the Ukraine. If we wanted to retain our Polish nationality, they would help us return to the German-occupied part of Poland. After what we had heard and experienced of the Soviet dictatorship, the thought of Soviet citizenship was not very appealing. Of course, we had no news of what was going on in the Polish ghettos; in fact, rumours were circulating that life under the Germans was not as bad as we had feared.

Many refugee families debated long and hard about what to do. In the end, most of the Jewish refugees registered to return to German-occupied Poland. So we eagerly looked forward to returning to our home in Rozwadów.

5. Exiled to Siberia

NOT LONG AFTER WE REGISTERED to return to Poland, a curfew was called in Lvov. We had to wait in our house. Eventually, some soldiers came by with an officer of the secret police. They ordered us to come with them in ten minutes. It was a hot summer day and we loaded everything we still had onto a truck waiting outside. Then we sat with 40 or so other people on top of the baggage and we were taken to the train station.

There were soldiers everywhere. We were sorted somehow into waiting freight trains – about forty wagons with fifty or sixty people in each wagon. The boxcar had an elevated platform with a primitive hole for use as a toilet; it may have been screened off by a kind of partition. Ours was not the only train; I saw others, and I have heard that nearly three hundred thousand people were transported that day.

When everyone was loaded, the freight cars were locked shut and the train moved away. It was hot and stuffy with only a small opening to peer through. We were all terribly thirsty and there was nothing to drink. We were locked in those wagons for two or three days, but it didn't take long to realize that we were not heading towards Poland, but deeper into Russia.

After some days, they at least opened the cars from time to time and let us out to find some food and water. I don't think Milech and Rahel were with us in the same boxcar, but they must have been in the same train because we all ended up in the same place. Finally after about two weeks in the boxcar, we arrived in a Siberian town called Sosva. There we were ordered off the train and we were sent several kilometres down the River Sosva. Several more kilometres inland, we found about one hundred log houses arranged in two double rows; this was Camp Forty-Five where we were to settle.

On our arrival, the Commandant of the camp addressed us from a platform. He spoke Russian and somebody translated. He said, 'You probably think that you won't stay here long. But I have been here twenty five years and I can assure you that I have never seen anyone leave this place. You had better get used to it. If you do, you will survive; otherwise you will perish.' That was our reception. We were now in 'forced exile', a status only slightly better than that of the infamous Siberian labour camps.

At that time, we were still disappointed that we had been tricked and sent to Siberia instead of to Poland as promised. But ironically, our longing to return to Poland probably saved our lives. The Jewish people who chose to remain in the Soviet Union were re-located in the Western

Ukraine. Most of them were later murdered when the Germans invaded, while those of us who tried to return to Poland were by then removed to the relative safety of Western Siberia. It was one of those times when God somehow used our own foolishness to protect us.

The log houses of the camp had been built by former exiles. Every log house had two rooms, and every family was to get one room. My father immediately set about making the best of the situation. He first tried to occupy one of the best houses in the centre of the camp, but we were soon evicted and told that it was reserved for privileged people. So we ended up in the very last house in one row.

Our one room was about five metres square with an old-fashioned Russian wood stove in one corner. My father built a platform for us to sleep on and he bartered with other refugees for some bricks to improve the stove for heating and cooking. By the time he added a table and primitive bench, the arrangement was reasonably comfortable.

Our next concern was to gather food and fuel for the winter. Mother took us two younger ones into the forests to gather cranberries. They were plentiful and we gathered hundreds of litres of cranberries. Father made a box in a shed outside to dry and store the berries for winter. We also worked very hard to gather a supply of firewood to keep us warm through the long Siberian winter. Because of Father's foresight and resourcefulness, we managed better than many other families. Some in the camp later starved or froze when the harsh Siberian winter set in.

Dense forest surrounded the settlement and the men's main work was cutting firewood. They cut, split and stacked the wood. Officials would come around measuring the stacks and calculating wages. Corruption was rampant. Sometimes an official would say, 'Give me a bottle of vodka and you can move this same pile to another place. I will write down that you did double.'

Some men worked near our house sawing wood. One man stood on a platform and they sawed up and down. My father also split firewood for a time, but then he found something better. Near our cabin at the end of the row were the stables for the officers' horses, wagons and sleighs. My father was given a wage to care for the animals and equipment. The officers would come any time, day or night, and tell him to hitch up a horse, or they would return a horse that needed to be fed and watered. This was much better work than splitting wood. So it worked out for the best that we had the house at the end of the row.

In early autumn, word went round that all men and all single women were to report for work at another camp several kilometres away near the river. Father didn't have to go because of his work with the horses, but Leo and Lena did. We didn't trust the Russians and we thought we would never see them again. But they actually did return after helping with the hay harvest.

There was a store in that place and we were free to buy whatever was available. The wages were actually enough to live on – as long as there was something to buy. But as the war progressed, food rations were cut smaller and smaller until hardly anything was left. My father, however, was not to be outdone. We were not allowed to go more that a few kilometres from the camp, but there was a collective nearby. My father knew how to strike deals with those remote peasants. I remember going with my father once to a farmer's wife at the collective. He took along an old apron that we had brought from Rozwadów. I thought it was just a worthless rag, but my father made it look quite nice. He made his sales pitch and finally the peasant woman asked what he wanted for it. My father coolly answered: 'fifty kilogrammes of potatoes, three litres of milk and some bread.' I was so embarrassed that I had to leave the room; I couldn't believe he could ask so much for that old apron. But a few minutes later, he came out with the precious food. We had quite a job to carry it all back to camp.

Mother stayed home and took care of us children as well as caring for the house. We had to go several hundred metres to fetch water from a spring. I had to do that task many times, even my younger sister did it. By then, I was eleven and she was nine. Especially when Mother did the laundry, we had to carry lots of water. We boiled the clothes and I helped with scrubbing them on the washboard and rinsing them out.

As I think back now, I wish I had helped more. There was so much work to do and my mother suffered excruciating pain from an untreated hernia. At some point, I started school and started learning to read and write

Russian. Interestingly, the peasant children walked the five kilometres through the frozen forest to come to school at our camp, because their collective was too poor to have its own school.

Our first months had been very hot. Clouds of bloodthirsty mosquitoes had tormented us while we picked berries and we had to be careful not to sink into swampy mires. But in winter, the landscape was transformed. By October or November, everything was frozen solid. Work and school continued as normal unless temperatures dropped below -50°C. My brother and sister came back from the woods each day completely encased in a frozen cocoon of rags. They had to sit quite a while by the stove before they were even able to peel off their clothing. Lena still has trouble with her feet from the frostbite damage. The father of the family next door caught pneumonia and died.

When spring finally came, we planted potatoes. My mother and I did most of the garden work: turning the soil and hauling manure the two to three hundred metres from the stalls where my father worked. We also had to haul the water for the garden. The potatoes grew well and by the end of summer, we were able to harvest a ten-fold return: one and a half tonnes of potatoes – enough to last for a year.

One day in the spring of 1941, Father came back from his morning chores and said that he was feeling unwell. He was a bit confused. He lay down and soon he was lying there completely unconscious, drooling out of his mouth.

Mother was beside herself and didn't know what to do. She called to the men who were sawing wood near our house and they ran for help. One of the refugees was a doctor and she helped the official Russian 'doctor' who had some medical training, although he was certainly no doctor. In any case, the doctor came and prodded Father's feet with needles, but there was no response. She confirmed that he had had a stroke and at that point it was unclear if he would recover. It was a terrible situation for Mother.

Leo and Lena were working quite some distance away at another camp, so one man went over to tell them what had happened. He found my sister and told her that father was not well, but at first she did not grasp the seriousness of what he was saying. Finally, he told her: 'Your father may be dying.' She quickly went to find Leo and they both slipped away and ran the ten to twelve kilometres to our house. Of course, by leaving their work, they risked being sent to forced labour camps.

They arrived at home around midnight. In all that time, Father had shown no signs of regaining consciousness. But just before they arrived he started to stir. What a relief they had to burst in and find that Father was still alive. This experience strengthened a real sense of unity in our family. It also brought us close to the two men who sawed near our house. They were both well-educated; one was an engineer, I think. They had also run quite a risk by leaving their work. In the end, though, no one was punished. My brother and sister returned to their work the next day. The foreman knew what had happened and turned a blind eye while the others covered for Leo and Lena.

By morning, Father was able to respond a little. Then he slept all day, still drooling out of his mouth. Finally, he woke up, looked around, and recognized us. So he was unconscious for a little less than twenty four hours. He may have been hindered on one side of his face, but very soon he was able to stand on his own feet. He was definitely weaker, but he was not seriously disabled. There was no medication for high blood pressure, but Mother watched him like a hawk to make sure that he didn't get too excited.

By the end of our second summer in Siberia, we heard that the Germans had invaded Russia. At first we worried what this news might mean for us, but it actually brought unexpected relief. Stalin was forced to turn to the Allies for help, and the Polish government in exile used this opportunity to demand the release of Polish refugees held in Siberia. Suddenly we heard that we were free to go as we wished! But of course we were still in the backwoods of Siberia and our homes in Poland were still under German occupation.

Father managed to rent a room in the little town of Sosva about twelve kilometres from camp. This town had a railway station, a post office, and a sawmill where Leo and Lena got jobs. We still had our year's supply of potatoes, so we made many trips back and forth carrying everything to Sosva.

We wanted to get out of Siberia and away from the advancing German army. Looking at a map, we picked

Uzbekistan in the south as the place to go. We thought that if the Germans took all of Russia, we could flee south through Afghanistan and eventually get to Palestine. We decided to eat the potatoes and save the rations of bread, since it would be easier to travel with bread. So we dried the bread in the hot sun and ate potatoes with cranberry sauce. We didn't have sugar, so the cranberries were very bitter. We also didn't have any meat, nothing but potatoes – morning, midday and evening. For several weeks we had that diet. But strangely enough, I still enjoy potatoes! Finally, we were able to join up with some other families and hire a boxcar. By November 1941, we were ready for our journey south.

6. Samarkand – Hunger and Disease

MANY DIFFERENT TRAINS TOOK our freight car along a tortuous route from Siberia to Uzbekistan. As we headed south, trains full of young soldiers were going the opposite direction – towards the front. Of course, military transports always had priority, so our wagon often stood several days at some station or another. We used these stops to find food and provisions for the journey, but we never knew when our train might start to move.

Once Leo and Lena were returning from some errand when the train suddenly started to pull away. Leo jumped into a wagon near ours, but it took all Lena's efforts to catch hold of the very last wagon. The Russian guard thought she was jumping the train and tried to push her off. She managed to hang on the end of the train and argue with him to the next station, where she jumped down and found us. We heard stories of such incidents where families were scattered.

We first tried to find refuge in Tashkent, the capital of Uzbekistan, but the city was completely overcrowded. After a few days, we made our way further south to Samarkand, but the situation there was no better. Hundreds of thousands of refugees were fleeing the German onslaught. Many were Jews, but many were not. Father finally managed to rent a room from a Buchara Jew. Our room was small: perhaps two metres by three metres. The six of us just managed to stretch out on the packed clay floor; we were like sardines in a tin.

We shared a courtyard and outdoor toilets with the Buchara Jews who lived in that compound. The language and customs of these people were strange to us. Even their synagogue was different from what we were used to in Eastern Europe. Later, I heard some speak ill of the Buchara Jews. It may be that some took advantage of the refugees, but on the whole they showed our family greater hospitality than might have been expected under such circumstances. The people were mostly poor themselves and must have suffered even more under the burden of our overcrowding.

Constant burning hunger gnawed at us through all those months in Samarkand; I had never experienced such desperate hunger. In order to get anything you had to stand in queues – sometimes overnight. Masses of people waited and pushed forward to collect tiny bread rations. People were crazy with hunger. Desperate people often attacked those who had collected their ration, snatching the bread and tearing at it on the spot like ravenous wolves. A gang of boys once hit me over the head and stole the bread I was carrying home.

Rumours occasionally made the rounds that a certain shop was expecting a delivery of some commodity or another. People would crowd to wait for hours outside the shop, often in the middle of the night. It was illegal to meet outside at night and the police would brutally disperse the crowds with sticks. But as soon as the police disappeared, everyone crowded back to wait outside the shop. This procedure might repeat itself two or three times during the night. When the shop finally opened, masses of people pressed in. I was small and developed quite some skill at worming my way to the front. Sometimes, I was trying to buy a bit of extra food; sometimes, it was brandy or some other scarce commodity that we could re-sell on the black market.

So somehow we managed to get enough food to survive. Many others simply died of starvation, or of the typhus epidemics that raged through the crowded quarters. Trucks would pass through the streets each day to collect the dead. Leo was the first in our family to have typhus. He had always been a healthy boy, but quite suddenly he came down with a high fever and hallucinations. Mother took care of him; I remember seeing her crying. At great expense, we managed to get a doctor. We tried desperately to keep him out of the overcrowded hospitals where the authorities isolated those with typhus. People were mostly just left there to die.

Then my mother caught the disease – probably from

Leo. We were determined to keep Mother out of the hospital. We were prepared to sell everything to pay for a doctor and medicines. We even stood guard at the door in case the health inspectors came near; then we would lock the door and pretend no one was at home. But Mother's condition only worsened. Worrying for us more than for herself, she sometimes cried out: 'What will happen to my children and my husband?' We were all gathered around her bed the night she died. It was the second day of Passover, the anniversary of Leo's birth.

Mother's death changed our lives forever. Her quiet loving care had held our family together through all those struggles. She actually spent herself in sacrifice for us. Often she gave up her portion of food so that I could have more. She often needed more help and support than I gave her. How I have since wished to re-live those days, to serve her as she served us. But there was only one last service we could do. We went together and buried her in the Jewish cemetery. My father chiselled her name onto the gravestone.

As half-orphans, Judith and I could now go to the Polish orphanage. Father thought we would be better cared for there, so we went. Although we were Polish by nationality and understood the language, we could never really feel at home among those Polish Catholics. Their prayers only reminded us of the pogroms through the Jewish quarters of Rozwadów. It also seemed to us that they prayed to statues – idols in our eyes – so we kept a wary distance.

Our standard of living was definitely higher in the orphanage. We had clean clothes and more food. But I did not thrive there. After I had glutted myself the first few times, my appetite dropped off. I began to feel sick in the night. I became emotionally numbed and began to focus only on survival. I must have turned thirteen in that orphanage, but I don't think I even noticed at the time. My *bar mitzvah* was lost in the inner and outer turmoil of those last weeks in Samarkand.

Teheran Children

7. The Teheran Children

IN AUGUST 1942, THE POLISH government in exile made efforts to evacuate Polish orphans from Russia. Many had already died from starvation and epidemics and the rest were barely surviving. Among some ten thousand evacuated children, there must have been eight hundred to one thousand Jewish children. We heard at the orphanage about this chance to get out and we debated among ourselves what we should do. It was not an easy decision, because it meant that I might never see any of my family again. Later I reproached myself for having left my father.

We were put in trains and brought to Krasnovodsk, a town in Turkmenistan on the Caspian Sea. There we were loaded onto ships. We must have been ten thousand people on that ship and we were packed in like sardines. There were no cabins or anything; we just lay on the deck or under the deck. I don't know how long we were on that ship – maybe thirty six hours. Then we came to a port called Pahlavi in Persia (Iran). It was summer, so we camped on the sandy beach.

For the first time in many months, we had proper food: mostly corned beef and concentrated milk from America. But by then I was already sick and didn't have any appetite. The Jewish Agency came around this camp looking for Jewish children. They were starting to gather Jewish children in Teheran, hoping to get them to Palestine. The Allies constantly sent supplies to Russia via Teheran and the Caspian Sea, so many trucks went back empty from Pahlavi to Teheran.

We were loaded onto these trucks – about ten to fifteen children in each. The roads were treacherous, very steep, with few passing places, and our way was littered with wrecks. As the truck lurched along these mountain tracks, I felt increasingly sick, I couldn't stop vomiting and my stomach hurt terribly. I was screaming with pain, I felt so bad that I tried to throw myself off the truck, but thankfully someone held me back.

It must have taken more than a day to get to Teheran, because we stopped for the night somewhere along the way. Near Teheran, a Polish military camp had one section for Jewish orphans. We were divided up into groups according to age and gender, so I lived with about forty to fifty boys in a big tent, where we slept on mats. In the centre of this Jewish camp was a combination store and kitchen where food was provided.

I had constant diarrhoea and still had no appetite. I weighed less than thirty kilogrammes and was very weak. I was just skin and bones and looked like the pictures we see now of children in the Third World. I looked so pitiful that the Jewish Agency took me around to the wealthy Jews in Teheran to arouse their sympathy and raise funds.

Otherwise, I just roamed the camp listlessly or sat with my sister Judith, pouring out my agony. I began to accuse myself of mistreating my mother and abandoning my father. I had nightmares and even said that I wanted to die. But Judith was always faithful to me and tried to encourage me. She was only eleven years old and I was thirteen, but I don't know how I would have survived without her. Therefore I remain deeply thankful for how she stood by me.

The Jewish Agency tried to organize us, to provide cultural activities, and to educate us a bit. For every fifty children there were some counsellors and there was somebody who was responsible for the whole camp. They were not all from Palestine: some were also refugees, who had somehow managed to get out of Russia. They were in contact with the Jewish Agency from Palestine who were trying to help us emigrate. We had no school while we were there, but the guidance counsellors taught us songs as we sat around the fire in the evening. Some of the songs I still know today, like '*Arim dem Fajer*'.

Among the counsellors was a man from Rozwadów and he recognized me. When he saw what state I was in, he brought me to Frau Zipporah Shertok, whose husband later became Prime Minister of Israel. At that time, she was responsible for the Jewish Orphanage in Teheran, Beit ha-Yeled ha-Yehudi. He showed her the skin peeling on the back of my legs and spoke with her in Hebrew, which I didn't understand. They established somehow that I had pellagra, a skin disease caused by a lack of meat in the diet. Along with another weak boy, I was allowed into the camp store and we could help ourselves to anything we liked. We could also order anything we wanted from the soldier's canteen. I always ordered hamburgers and potatoes, and soon I began to gain weight.

But before long I was sick again and was sent to hospital. They suspected scabies, which was going around the camp, so I was put in isolation. While I was there, news came that we would all be travelling to Palestine. I was terrified that I would be left behind and begged to be released. Just a day or two before the group left, I finally got out.

We had arrived in Teheran in August 1942 and stayed there for about six months. Then we left for Palestine. The quickest way would actually have been over land through

Iraq, but Iraq wouldn't let us go through, so we had to take a roundabout way to Palestine. We traveled in a train to a port on the Arabian Sea. Then we were loaded onto a military transport ship bound for Karachi in India (now Pakistan). We travelled in a convoy of fifteen to twenty ships and we were constantly on alert that we might have to abandon ship. This was toward the end of 1942, so there was intense fighting with the Japanese. Planes sometimes came close to the ships and it was very frightening.

On the ship we slept in hammocks, many children all around. I remember eating marmalade for the first time and we learned some English songs from the British soldiers. Years later when living with English people, I tried to sing 'My Bonnie Lies over the Ocean.' They enjoyed it tremendously because I mixed up all the words. Of course, the sounds meant nothing to me, but that was my first contact with English.

I don't remember too much about Karachi except that it was very hot. We stayed in a camp on the outskirts of Karachi and undoubtedly learned more songs and dances from our counsellors. By this time I had a big appetite, but everything was rationed so I was always hungry. After three to four weeks, we put to sea again and sailed up past Aden, through the Red Sea, and eventually landed at the town of Suez. From there we travelled by train to Palestine.

Teheran Children arrive in Palestine

8. Palestine

I ARRIVED IN PALESTINE in February 1943. It seemed like the whole country was waiting for us and we were received with open arms. As our train from the Suez Canal passed through each station, there were delegations of children and others with flowers, holding them up and greeting us. We were called the Children of Teheran. I don't think we were called that in Teheran, but that is what they called us in Palestine.

The train from Suez took us to a temporary absorption camp called Atlit – about twenty kilometres south of Haifa. Most of us were used to living as street children.

Even during the journey, some of the children had been stealing and getting into all kinds of mischief. We were a rough lot – quite a challenge for our carers. But they showed us a lot of love and slowly they gained our trust. Later on, I think they realized themselves that they had been a little too naïve. Thinking of us as poor children, they didn't demand the discipline that they might have. Whenever some food was put on the table, the children would grab as much as they could, and hide some to have later or to barter. When they gave out clothing, if the person handing it out turned around, some children would come back and say, 'I didn't get any' so that they could get more. My most vivid memory of Atlit was a mountain of oranges. None of us could believe that we could eat as many oranges as we liked. We ate until we were nearly sick.

My dream was coming true; I was actually in *Eretz Yisrael.* It was a tremendous relief to find ourselves in complete safety, but we were also worried about our loved ones – especially our families. We didn't think much about bigger political issues at that time. Like most of the other children, I spent the first year or two in Israel trying to work through all my experiences of the war. I had nightmares and often woke in the night screaming. I was quite nervous and easily lost my temper. It was no different with the other children.

The children ranged in age from one to fifteen. So it was a big job to sort us out. First they tried to identify the various health problems that were rampant among us: lice, scabies, malnutrition, etc. We were sent to different places for recuperation. Judith and I went to Jerusalem, and lived in a girl's boarding school called Beit Tseerot Mizrachi. The girls vacated that place and spent 6-8 weeks in a kibbutz to make room for us. There we were provided with new clothing and food. They took us out for tours in a bus. We visited a kibbutz and different sites in Jerusalem and all over Israel.

After six to eight weeks of recuperation, they started to decide where we should all go. The mother of *Youth Aliyah*, the youth immigration movement, was a famous Jewish-American lady called Henrietta Szold. She was quite old, but she had these young children on her heart and she made a point of interviewing each one of us. She asked us about our parents' background, what they would have wished for us.

They asked Judith and me if our parents were religious orthodox, and we told them they were. In the end, they sent us to a cooperative village called Moshav Sde Yaacov. This was a modern orthodox Zionist village. They were religious, but not like the Hasidic Jews with beards and side locks. They were mostly shaven and they were very Zionist, very dedicated people. I also went to school there and learnt Hebrew. This was new. Some of us had learned written Hebrew already in Poland, but none of us knew how to speak it.

My friend at that time was Jakob Finkelstein, a boy maybe a year older than me. The first contact we had was while playing chess as we travelled on the ship to Karachi. Somehow we got into a fist fight and I had a bloody nose.

But after that fight we started a friendship that lasted for many years. We spent many hours talking together and also stood up for each other – though I think it was mainly Jakob who took it on himself to protect me in the first months. Jakob also had a sister, Zahava, who was my sister Judith's best friend. Jakob was much more world savvy than I was, and knew how to get the most out of any situation. But it was interesting: on the one hand, he could take advantage of others in a very shrewd, almost cynical way; on the other hand, he was a very faithful friend to me.

In the boarding school in Jerusalem, Jakob discovered that there was a telephone, something quite unknown to us boys at that time. So he wanted to try it out and see how it worked. He looked up addresses and found some religious organizations and just for fun he phoned them and told them, 'We are being brainwashed here. They are forcing us to give up our religious faith. Can you please help us?' This is the sort of prank we boys used to play.

Jakob and his sister Zahava were also assigned to Moshav Sde Yaacov along with Judith and me. I was still very nervous and had not found my feet, so I encountered quite a few problems. I was first with one family, but I didn't get along with the mother of the house. They soon put me with another family, but there I had a confrontation with a hired man. He was basically running the farm because the son of the family was fighting with the Jewish Brigades. This man was a refugee from Hungary, in his 40's. He was tall and strong, a good farmer – and he was very religious.

During the time before New Year called *Sleekhot*, religious people get up in the morning and have a special time of prayer to seek forgiveness for wrongs they may have done through the year. Now this man tried to force me to get up very early, three or four o'clock in the morning and go with him to the synagogue. The first day, I refused to get up. The next day he poured cold water on me to wake me up, but still I refused. As we sat around the table at supper that evening he said, 'Now Josef, tomorrow if you don't get up I'm going to do it again.' I got in a rage, I had a knife and I threw it at him. I lost my temper completely. I threw myself on the floor, and I made a terrific scene. I was shouting, 'You're not my father, you have no rights over me.' They were really frightened. Eventually I quieted down, but from that point on he didn't talk with me anymore. I continued to help on the farm, but he ignored me.

Why did I start to rebel against the Jewish religion? I think part of it was my picture of a strict God who will punish us. I felt guilty for my mother's death and for leaving my father in the Soviet Union. I was afraid.

In any case, many of us were unhappy at the co-operative settlement. After 8 months, we sent a delegation to Jerusalem and expressed that we were not happy. They decided to send the older ones away, and the younger ones stayed. I went with the older ones, fourteen to fifteen years, to the agriculture school at Mikveh Israel. So Jakob and I left Moshav Sde Yaacov, but Judith and Zahava stayed there for about three years.

Josef & Jakob

9. At the School of Agriculture

MIKVEH ISRAEL IS SAID TO BE the oldest Zionist settlement in Palestine, though there were some Jews living among the Arabs before that. Charles Netter, a Jewish philanthropist from France founded it in 1870 to train young people in agriculture. This settlement later became the most renowned agricultural school in the whole of the Middle East. Besides teaching the students, the extensive farm covered all areas of agriculture: a dairy with sixty to eighty cows, sheep, and an orchard with all kinds of trees. They even had a botanical garden with many rare plants.

In the school were two sections: the religious section

made up mostly of immigrant students like ourselves, and the secular section made up mostly of students from kibbutzim and cooperatives. These secular Jews were the majority of the Jewish population in Israel at the time. The two groups lived separately and had separate classes although it was all in one school.

The Children of Teheran were together as one group within the religious group. We had a two-year course. Each student had a chance to work in all the branches of agriculture in the first year, and then in the second year we could specialize in one area for six months, and a secondary branch for a further three months.

Our teachers were also our guidance counsellors and tried to help us. Most of them were modern Orthodox Jews from religious kibbutzim. I made their lives hard – I was restless and often a disturbance in class. At the same time I started to ask many questions, also about faith. On the one hand, I was still rebelling against my idea of a strict God, but I was also beginning to grapple with the Holocaust – to ask why God had allowed that to happen. Some of the other children had come almost directly from the concentration camp of Buchenwald. They started to tell about what had happened in Germany. These children were our age, maybe even younger, but they looked like old men: the way they talked and the way they acted. All of us were shaken up by this.

In the beginning of 1944 around April, our whole class from Mikveh went to Kibbutz Tirat Zvi, a religious kibbutz in the valley of Beit Sha'an. The kibbutz had a workcamp: we lived in tents and worked there for about two months. One day I was standing in line to get food and started talking with a boy who was a few years older than I, maybe eighteen or twenty. When I told him that I was from Frankfurt and that my name was 'Nacht', he said that he knew my family. I asked him his name and when he told me, I immediately said, 'I remember you, you had a candy shop! It was around the corner from where we lived.' He said, 'Sure enough!' It's actually amazing because I couldn't have been older than four when we left Frankfurt.

This was my first experience living on a kibbutz, but kibbutz life didn't impress me much at that time. I was still trying to cope with the experiences of the war, the memories of Russia and Iran. When we told people what we had experienced in Russia, they simply wouldn't believe us. They didn't want to believe what we told them. There was a terrific sympathy toward the Soviet Union, because they were fighting against Hitler. They also had an idealistic picture of what was happening in Russia, the land of socialists.

When we returned to Mikveh, some of the other students started a group (*hachsharah*) with the idea of starting a kibbutz. They eventually joined Kibbutz Kfar Ezion which is south of Jerusalem. (During Israel's war of independence, the Jordanian legions overran their kibbutz, so many of them lost their lives later or were captured.) Some of my fellow classmates were part of this group, but I was against it. I couldn't accept their religiosity and I was just too rebellious.

At about this time, I made a conscious decision to oppose religion altogether. I said that I didn't believe in God, I didn't believe in a supernatural power, I wasn't going to accept anything that I couldn't grasp with my head. I had many questions and we had heated discussions in class.

As *Yom Kippur,* Atonement Day, approached, everyone in the religious group prepared for the fasts, but as a consequence of the convictions I felt at the time, I decided as a fifteen-year-old to break with that also. That was no small thing: among religious people, *Yom Kippur* is an awesome experience. But I decided that I wouldn't fast on *Yom Kippur*, I would switch on the lights and drink whatever I wanted. I wouldn't have anything to do with it anymore. When I felt something was right, then I felt I had to do it – not just talk about it – and then accept the consequences.

I was very much alone during this time, except for my friend Jakob. Jakob was in the class below me, but we were still together and we talked a lot together. We decided that when we had finished our course we would go out together and help one another. But Jakob was more pragmatic than I was. He also became secular, but he just wanted to make a go of it in society. He didn't buck the system like I did. I made life hard for myself by following my ideals.

At one point, I was even violent against this group that was going to the kibbutz. We lived together in a dorm, but the boys in this group stuck together and ignored me. One day, I went up to one of their ringleaders and I hit him hard in rage. He was quite shocked, because it was completely unexpected. I heard afterwards that they were planning to gang up on me and take revenge. Some friends found a way to shelter me in the secular part of Mikveh. So I stayed there a couple of nights until things quieted down. But at school they were convinced that I was a bad influence. They managed to convince me that I should leave on my own. I was actually only a few months short of completing the two-year course.

They actually prohibited Jakob and me to be together. Jakob stayed at the school, but we still met in the dark. We walked together and decided that we were going to stick together. I would go out and find a job, and earn some money, and then he would come out and we would make it together. We would pool our income. Neither of us were interested in agriculture. He wanted to become an electrician, which he eventually did.

There was another Polish boy at Mikveh named Benjamin Bodner, who had escaped from a train travelling to a concentration camp, and then found his way to Israel. He was also unhappy at the school and we had talked together about leaving. He told me about the Palmach, the most elite group in the Haganah, the Jewish resistance army. He thought we should enlist in this group, so we went together. Maybe I thought there was some glamour in it, but I was not very motivated. He was accepted and I wasn't. I don't know why I was rejected, but I was very high-strung and I was also a year younger than Benjamin.

He was later killed during the last days of the war of independence. His father survived concentration camp and came to Israel only to find that his son had been killed.

At Mikveh Israel, we had been trained in weaponry. We learned how to assemble rifles and revolvers. We practiced target shooting. We learned how to climb and jump over houses and held exercises as if we were attacked. We even went out into the desert together and did different military exercises. At that time, there was a lot of trouble with the Bedouins. They used sticks as weapons, so we learned how to fight with sticks – how to hit and how to defend ourselves. Through that training, I was already an unofficial member of the Haganah, but when I left the school I lost contact with them for the time being.

Aunt Elsa, Judah,
Uncle Chaim Simcha, Sammy

10. The Search Begins

WHEN I LEFT MIKVEH, I looked for a job. One of the things that I had specialized in at Mikveh was dairy. With some help from the college, I got a job at a dairy farm not far from Tel Aviv. The farmer delivered milk into Tel Aviv with his horse and wagon. People started work early because of the heat, so he had to deliver milk early in the morning while people were still at home. In the summer I had to get up at one o'clock and milk the cows. In the winter it was three o'clock. He gave me room and board and some small wage. That was my first job and I was very happy to be on my own.

I worked at that dairy farm for about four months, and at first things went well. But then I got into a conflict with the farmer's wife and had to leave abruptly. I told her I couldn't work for her, so again I was looking for a job.

I had some relatives in Israel. My Uncle Chaim Simcha is a younger brother of my mother, and was very close to her. Partly because of his love for my mother, he also had a great love for me. He had seen on the list of Teheran Children that my sister and I were coming. So when I first arrived at Atlit, he came to find us. As we sat in the bus to go to Jerusalem, he was suddenly there beside the bus and we talked through the window. He was that kind of a person, very warm and dedicated. Of course, he asked about my mother, but I was not very sensitive. I told him there and then that my mother was not living any more, and he had a terrific shock.

The home of Uncle Chaim and Aunt Elsa became a kind of second home for me. Whenever I had time off in Mikveh or at the cooperative, I could just come to their house. I felt at home there and they received me like a son. Chaim Simcha was an extraordinary man with a broad view of the world. He was religious, but he was considered in his circles to be open-minded and a deep thinker. He was a well respected person and people often came to him for advice about personal matters or problems in the village.

But even more than Chaim Simcha, it was his son Sammy who influenced me deeply. Sammy was five years older than I, but he always treated me as his friend and equal. When I left the dairy farm, I turned to Sammy for help. I hadn't only lost my job, I had lost my room as well. Sammy had his own place in Tel Aviv; he let me live with him and he helped me find a place of my own. He shared everything with me and didn't make a big thing of it. That generous spirit impressed me very much.

Being there, I also met many of his friends. Sammy must have been part of one of the underground groups which had formed to fight the British. When the terrorist action started against the British, the British jumped on everyone connected with these groups. Sammy was arrested, but I don't think they found anything against him. He was sent to detention camp as many were, but then was released and kept on the list as one of the sympathizers. He was under house arrest and had to register with the police every day. During that time, many of his friends came to visit him at his house.

Over the following years I had many, many discussions with Sammy and his friends that changed my outlook on life. Sammy did not live for himself. He inspired me to have a bigger vision, to think of others' needs and of the whole world.

At that time I also started reading and thinking, especially about the struggle for justice and for brotherhood, about the meaning of life – that one must live for something beyond oneself. I had learned Hebrew when I was fourteen to fifteen years old, and I can't remember reading any books before that. But now I went to the library often. I read all of Tolstoy's and Dostoyevsky's books that were in Hebrew. I bought and read 'Crime and Punishment' in one night. I couldn't have taken it all in, but certainly something stayed with me. The French author, Romain Rolland, influenced me greatly with his ideals of friendship and social justice – particularly his story of Antoinette and Olivier, two orphan children who supported one another through hard times. This inspired me in my efforts to join forces with Jakob, who by then had also left Mikveh Israel and had found a job.

Eventually I found some lodging and work and Jakob came to join me. I earned £20 a month and rented a place for £10, so I could put aside the other £10 as savings. We shared all the money we earned in a common purse. I wasn't so concerned about money, but Jakob was more prudent. Eventually we gave up the common purse and divided up the money equally between us, so that none of us had more than the other.

We worked hard, but we also had a lot of fun together. Once Jakob boasted that he could eat two dozen eggs at one sitting, but I didn't believe he could. So I said that if he could eat two dozen eggs, then I would pay for them. He readily agreed, so we went into a shop and bought eggs. I especially ordered extra large eggs and some bread to go with it – by this time, I was starting to get a little nervous. Jakob ate the eggs, bread and all. I lost my bet!

During that whole time when I was sixteen and

seventeen, I was really grappling with the meaning of life. What is the purpose of it all? I didn't have a faith, but I was also not satisfied just living for myself. Jakob was busy trying to make a good living and having a good time. However, I thought there was no point in living just to make money and gain recognition. I could see that these things don't make people happy. So we continued to live together, but we drifted slowly apart.

Instead, I was drawn closer and closer to Sammy and his friends. I particularly remember Isaiah and Channah, an engaged couple with whom we discussed many issues. We weighed up the relative advantages of capitalism, socialism and communism. These issues had real meaning for us as we considered the political situation in Israel – the different parties and their differing ideologies.

Sammy also influenced me in personal moral issues. He was an example of practical caring for others, but he also challenged people forthrightly whenever there was any kind of off-colour humour or any hint of impurity. His attitude really made me think about my own values in the sexual area. Actually, he taught me what it means to have reverence before the dignity of others, especially women. Just being in his room opened my horizon beyond the basics of having a job and being accepted by others. I began to look beyond the trivial day-to-day issues and to ask myself, what I wanted to live for.

I wanted to live for that which is right, no matter what the cost. But I was also torn in two. I felt very weak and incapable of living up to the ideals I was setting for myself.

But deep down, I knew that I could not give up this striving. It may have had something to do with my roots: the calling to live out the prophetic vision of brotherhood, which I believe is deeply ingrained in the Jewish heart.

At the same time, the political situation in Palestine was very much on my mind. I was still trying to come to grips with what had happened in the Holocaust. The Holocaust was over and many survivors wanted to come to Palestine, but the British denied them entry. We constantly heard in the news about the ships that were apprehended by the British – thousands of people were turned away. They were taken to Cyprus and some were sent back to Europe. I hated the Germans, but now that the war was over, my hatred turned more and more towards the British.

It is remarkable, but I didn't see the Arabs as enemies – only the British. These feelings were widespread: many people shouted abuse at the British soldiers and different underground groups attacked them. British troops came through the towns in tanks and their police stations were like fortresses surrounded by razor wire.

At the same time, I was convinced that people could only be happy by living together in harmony with others. I dreamed of an ideal society where people would live together in peace. I knew that hate had no place in such a world. Nevertheless, I could not forget the Holocaust. I wanted to dedicate my life to fighting for the survival of our people. I was quite prepared to fight the British with any means.

With Sammy's help, I had found work doing different

odd jobs in and around Tel Aviv. I swept streets, dug holes, repaired roads, and did various kinds of building repair work. It was hard physical work. Then I met up with a group that did similar work for the town with a mule and wagon, so I got a job with them. I earned around £1.70 per day and worked six days a week, so that was quite a step up for me. When I got paid on Friday, I would usually go and buy books. I also read a lot from the newspapers as I sat in a café with my workmates while waiting for the next job. I was interested in all that was going on underground, but in general the news of the day enraged me more and more until I felt that I simply had to act.

11. Fighting for the Land

THERE WERE THREE ZIONIST underground organisations in Palestine at the time. The first was the Haganah, which later became the Israeli army. The Irgun (Irgun Zvai-Leumi or 'Military National Organization') was more radical and nationalistic, seeking to establish a Jewish State on both sides of the Jordan. Many of them were arrested by the British and some were executed for terrorist acts against the British. Then there was a smaller group called the Lechi (Lohamei Herut Yisrael or 'Freedom Fighters of Israel'). The British called it the Stern Group after its founder, Avraham Stern. This group saw the British as the principal enemies and attacked British targets wherever possible: military and civilian.

Since I had no family in Israel, I wanted to dedicate my life to fighting for the survival of our people. I was attracted to the Stern Group and wanted to join them, but I couldn't find a contact. I managed once to get into contact with the Irgun. I was led very secretively to a construction site somewhere and a strong light was trained on me so I could not see my questioners but they could see me. They asked me, 'Do you know what the goal of the Irgun is?' I was quiet. I wasn't so attracted to this whole idea of great national aspiration. My main thought was that we have to fight against British imperialism. So I was quiet and I didn't know what to answer. I also hadn't wanted to join them; I wanted to join the Stern Group. So they said, 'Shall we tell you what the goal of the Irgun is? A Jewish State on both sides of the Jordan. Do you agree with that?' I said I agreed. But it was obvious that I had failed. I must have been around seventeen at the time.

In November 1947 the vote came up in the United Nations about the partition of Palestine into an Arab State and a Jewish State. There was great expectation in the country about this vote. I remember many people standing in the streets of Tel Aviv listening to the radio as each country made its vote. It went on and on, and eventually I went to bed. I lived about three kilometres from the centre of Tel Aviv. But in the middle of the night I heard a loud commotion. I realized that the UN vote had gone in our favour, so I then got up and managed to get a taxi into Tel Aviv. The city was euphoric. There were thousands of people roaming the streets. Some of the shops opened and gave out free drinks; people stood and rejoiced. They were dancing around in the middle of the town.

I was in Tel Aviv for the rest of the night. By six or seven in the morning, the first casualties were reported. A bus from Jerusalem to Tel Aviv was attacked and many people were killed. Most of the Jewish part of Palestine agreed to the partition of the land, but most Arabs did not. They felt cheated and, of course, they were the majority of people in Israel at that time. They felt that the whole land belonged to them, and we were there as foreigners taking away part of their land. From this time on conflict started in earnest. The British accepted the decision of the United Nations and agreed to leave the country by 15 May 1948.

During this interim period from November 1947 to May 1948, the different underground organisations really began to mobilize. By then, the main fighting was between the Jews and the Arabs. The British were preparing to leave and mostly just let events take their own course. Occasionally they intervened on one side or the other. During most of 1948, Jewish and Arab groups were fighting all over the country to gain control of different towns and former British police stations.

I was keen to join in the military struggle. Never again could we accept it that millions of our people would be slaughtered as they were in the Holocaust. We would fight for the land of Israel and establish a safe homeland for our people. In February, I managed to enlist in the Haganah and fought in various conflicts until the ceasefire.

I didn't know at this time that my father had safely returned to Germany. I felt it was better that I die for such a cause than someone with parents and family, so I always tried to volunteer in the army for anything which looked dangerous. With this in mind, I was trained to use explosive mines and other things. I was no great expert in it, but I was in the explosives unit of the Alexandroni brigade in the 33rd battalion of the army.

Around May 1948 I finally managed to get in contact with the Stern Group. I was summoned to a nearby camp where I was blindfolded and interviewed. I told them my concern about the British Empire – that they would never allow a free and independent Jewish state. They accepted me and I came to fight with them. But when the State of Israel was declared a few days later, we were asked to return to our military units.

We were involved in many incidents, but the most serious was at a town called Kefar Sava. Part of the town was Jewish and part was Arab and our unit was to storm the Arab part. My unit went to lay mines and defend the road from the nearby town of Qalqilya and prevent any Arab reinforcements breaking through. The Arab resistance was much stronger than expected. Within minutes, many of our men were dead or injured. I have vivid memories of my comrades dying before my eyes. Our commanding officer ordered us to abandon the hill and retreat to a nearby orchard. Those of us who had not been hit tried to help the injured. Under heavy fire, we succeeded in moving some of our injured comrades to relative safety. But we were encircled by Arabs and isolated from our regiment.

Our commanding officer decided to take a small party back to Kefar Sava to ask for reinforcements. I went along to guide them through the mines I had laid. While we were gone, the Arabs attacked; they killed the wounded soldiers and mutilated their bodies. I reproached myself for leaving them there alone, even though there was nothing I could have done to save them. We were all shocked by that experience, but many were enraged and waited for some way to take revenge.

A few days or a week later we were in action trying to take the village of Tantura. This is maybe thirty kilometres south of Haifa, close to the sea. After some fierce fighting, we managed to take control of the town. There were rumours that some men from the village were killed in revenge for the massacre at Kefar Sava. I never saw any killing, but even the rumour had an effect on me. I wanted to fight for the right to live in this land. I was more than ready to fight against the armies of Egypt, Jordan and other countries. I was prepared to give my life to secure the existence of the State of Israel. But I was frightened to think that cruel hatred and bloodthirsty revenge could so easily take hold of men's hearts.

Of course, there was not time to think too deeply about such things. At the time, I only thought how I wanted to do more. In my unit was a young man name Schmuel Getter. He belonged to a group of young people preparing to start a kibbutz and he wanted to re-join the rest of this group who were all part of the Palmach, a more elite group in the army. For my part, I thought I would see more action with the Palmach. So we left our unit together and found the unit where his friends served. I didn't want to tell them that my name was Josef Nacht, because then they would find out that I actually belonged to a different unit, so I said my name is Josef Ben-Eliezer. Ben-Eliezer means the son of Eliezer, which was true. I did this on the spur of the moment and I have had that name ever since.

While I was with the Palmach, I was mostly together with Schmuel and his friends. These young men and women had everything in common. Even though they were in the army they lived like a community within the army. The women kept a supply of all the clothing; you could help yourself to the clothing you needed, and then give it back to be washed.

Our unit was heavily involved in the capture of Lod near Tel Aviv. Also here, my faith in human nature suffered a serious blow. After the town was conquered, there was some fighting on the streets, but then basically the entire Arab population was ordered to leave. I still remember vividly those long lines of refugees – men, women and children – fleeing towards an uncertain future. At one point, my unit was searching those who left the town for weapons and valuables. The atmosphere was tense and some of my comrades treated the Arabs spitefully. In that moment, my mind flashed back to my own experiences as a ten-year-old boy fleeing our home in Poland. But here the roles were reversed. One of my comrades struck a Palestinian with his bayonet and I was stung by the memory of my father being struck the same way by a German soldier. It shook me to the depths: how can men treat each other like that?

I saw two of our soldiers – actually just boys – take some Arabs and ask them to dig a grave. They ordered them to go in and took aim at them with their rifles. Several of us shouted at them and they let the men go, but I was shocked that we seemed quite capable of doing the same things that we heard from other nations. So still I was in turmoil. I wanted to fight for the State of Israel, but only because we were fighting for our survival, not to hurt people in a mean way. Those young men would have never done such a thing under normal circumstances, but we were in a situation where moral standards seemed thrown to the wind.

During that time I tried to help an Arab man who had been forced to dig trenches for us. He must have known some Hebrew, because I remember him telling me that he was a barber. I told him to go home, but he had lost his family among the crowds of people streaming out of town. Again I remembered how our family had fled Rozwadów and I felt somehow obliged to help him. I walked with him through the narrow streets of Lod carrying my Sten semi-automatic rifle. It was crazy really to be out alone like that; I could easily have been killed. In any case, we went right through the middle of town and finally found his family with all their possessions loaded on a horse wagon. I escorted them safely to the edge of town, but I have no clue what became of them afterwards. So there was a lot of suffering and even brutality, but there were also a few moments where kindness prevailed.

Shortly after the action at Lod I got quite sick. At first I didn't know what was wrong, but eventually the medics realized I had malaria. By that time, I was so exhausted, I could barely function. After a few weeks of quinine treatment in hospital I was able to re-join my comrades, but things were changing. A ceasefire had been declared and there was no more active fighting – at least for the time being. The atmosphere in the unit also shifted. We had always had a strong sense of comradeship; the officers and enlisted men were all in it together. But now, the Israeli army was starting to consolidate and they began to put more emphasis on formal military discipline. Training exercises were strict and mechanical. In any case, I was no longer so close to my friends in the Palmach unit, so I returned to my unit in the Alexandroni brigade. Of course I was arrested for desertion, but the officers were lenient because I had only been looking for tougher action. I was also begging to re-join my explosives unit that was just mobilizing for action in the Negev. This was towards the end of 1948 and was, I think, the last heavy action of the war.

Two villages in the Negev were still held by Egyptian units led by Gamal Abdul Nasser, who later became President of Egypt. My explosives unit had a new, untried weapon: a flame-thrower. We had several of them, but it was dangerous, mostly because none of us really knew how to use them. One of them was issued to a boy in my unit named David. He was obviously frightened and I knew he was the only son in his family. I volunteered to take it and our commanding officer agreed. Tragically, David was killed in the first onslaught against Iraq-Manshir. Meanwhile

I carried this useless, heavy flame-thrower all night in the pouring rain.

Sometimes I have felt guilty: maybe David would have lived if I had not taken his place. On the other hand, I am thankful for the miracle that I am still alive after deliberately putting myself in danger so many times. Because I was mostly in the explosives unit, I never actually killed anyone close up, but I was plagued with flashbacks of my comrades dying in battle. Pangs of guilt for my mother's death and my father's unknown fate haunted me still. I could not overcome this inner turmoil and the malaria only made things worse.

My sister Judith and others of my family really went out of their way to support me again during this very difficult time. I went to an army psychologist a few times and left the army in January 1949. Of course, most of the fighting was over by then and Israel was negotiating an armistice with the Arab countries.

Very soon after that I started to think about all we had done. We came to Israel and just wanted to live like anyone else – why shouldn't we have that right? But because we wanted to live, it meant that we directly or indirectly caused other people to be uprooted and to live in misery. I came more and more to the conclusion that I could never again cause harm to other people, no matter how noble the cause.

Josef, Father, Leo

12. A Reunion

AFTER I LEFT THE ARMY I suddenly came in contact with my father. Earlier my father had managed to get to Frankfurt from Samarkand. Along with my older brother and sister he went through post-war Poland and Austria and succeeded in getting to Germany. In the meantime both my brother and sister were married. My sister already had a daughter. They had all gone to Frankfurt to reclaim their property there. They also managed to get some restitution money.

My father invited me to come to Germany. In those days, it wasn't so easy to get to Germany – or even to

Europe – so no one knew when I would arrive. I managed to fly to Paris, and then on a small plane with fifteen to twenty people to Belgium, and then on to Frankfurt. This was the only connection to Frankfurt, you could not go from Paris. Many years later, I marvelled at the massive Frankfurt Airport; at that time the 'terminal' was just a small shack. I had only been able to take £10 out of Israel and I had spent most of that already. So I just asked for directions, shouldered my rucksack and hiked out to find my father's house.

I finally found Sandweg 46 and there was my father walking in front of the house. He had barely changed, but his pale, emaciated child from Samarkand had disappeared completely. He stopped and looked at me, wondering who was this tanned twenty-year old lingering in front of his house. I went to him and said, 'Father!' He embraced me. Then my brother and sister rushed out to join this tearful reunion after seven years of painful separation.

As a child, I had not been close to my father. We had often been in conflict as he vainly tried to tame my rebellious nature. In an instant, all that was washed away without any need to talk about it. He was prepared to do anything to help me. I remember how proudly he brought out an expensive gold watch that he had bought as a welcome present. Just to see my father, my brother and my sister alive helped me begin to overcome my feelings of guilt for having left them in Samarkand.

In the post-war confusion, my father had managed to set up a lucrative trade in cigarettes and other scarce commodities. He wanted me to join him, but in my idealism, I felt that I should live from my own work and not try to earn money by commerce. I wanted to learn a trade, so I found a job laying tiles. I stayed at this job for about six months until I stupidly twisted my ankle and had to stop work.

Just being in Germany was important for me. I hadn't met any Germans since my childhood and I had a picture of them as pathological maniacs or animals. How else could they have perpetrated the horrors of the Holocaust? But living and working with Germans began to soften this view. The master tile-layer I worked for was quite a nice person, a perfectly normal human being. It shook me to think that he could have been a Nazi, even in the SS. Clearly, people like Hitler and Himmler had deliberately committed their lives to evil, but what made so many German people accept this evil and even support it? I had to remember those two boys in Lod. What force unleashes such cruelty in the human heart? In situations where there is no moral constraint, human beings can become like pathological maniacs.

At the same time, I knew that I must never forget what happened in the Holocaust. Two of my cousins had died in a concentration camp; my mother and several other relatives had died of starvation and disease in Russia. I bought a book with photographs from different scenes from the Holocaust. I took it out many times, just to remember. Now these pictures are etched in my memory.

Fifty years afterwards, the pain of it sometimes

overwhelms me still. I had a few chances to go to the Holocaust Museum in Washington, but I couldn't bring myself to go. A few years ago, I visited the Diaspora Museum in Israel, but I could not stay; the pictures were more than I could bear. The pictures in my mind are already sometimes more than I can bear. I shudder not only for those who suffered, but also for those who have done those terrible things. I shudder that there is a power at work in the world that brings people to do such terrible things.

Judith and Josef

13. The Search Continues

I WAS IN GERMANY FOR ONE YEAR from August 1949 until 1950. I spent all that time with my father and my married brother and sister. But after my accident, I was at loose ends. I hadn't really found my feet in Germany, so I decided to return to Israel. I was by no means a convinced Zionist, but I felt more at home in Israel. For one thing, I knew the language. And I felt that I and the whole Jewish people had some purpose, some destiny to fulfil. I didn't believe in God, but I wanted to live for something bigger than myself.

Once back in Israel, I began to ask myself, 'Why do I always try to be different from everyone else?' I thought I should try to just conform with normal society like everybody else. I looked up my old friend Jakob Finkelstein who had always been much more a man of the world than I. We decided to start a business together. I had some money from my father and he had the business know-how. We bought a few ice cream machines and set up shop. Because I had been in the army, I was able to get the required rationing permits.

The business was quite a success, but after one summer I had enough of it. This was not the purpose of life I was seeking. We settled affairs between us and parted as friends. We were just different characters: Jakob was quite content to fit into society and get the most out of it, but I just couldn't be satisfied with a day-to-day trudge through life.

My whole inner struggle during this time is reflected in the books, plays, and films that affected me deeply. When Lennie loses control of himself and kills his friend in Steinbeck's 'Of Mice and Men', he seemed to me to cry out for the need of the whole human race. What is it that prevents people from living in harmony together? The same theme echoed for me through Sartre's 'No Exit' where three people are forced to live together and manage to make each other's lives miserable. At the end of the play, one character remarks, 'Hell is other people'. But nowhere is my burning question of that time more poignantly expressed than in Dostoyevsky's 'The Idiot', when Prince Myshkin makes his heart-rending cry: 'Why can people not live together? Why can they not listen to one another?'

More and more, I searched among ideals and idealists. The Zionist socialist movement didn't attract me. I felt that the atmosphere had changed from the early Kibbutz movement where young Zionists had to overcome all kinds of dangers and obstacles to eke out a living. During my time in the Palmach, I saw all those young people collecting the spoils of war for their new kibbutz. They talked about socialism and the brotherhood of mankind, but it looked like plundering to me. After that, I never even contemplated joining a kibbutz.

I started to read a lot of Marxist literature and I had many talks with Sammy. He convinced me more and more that the Palestinians would always hate us as part of the Zionist enterprise. In a way, he just confirmed my sense that our efforts to establish a homeland could only be realized by disrupting the lives of others. At the same time, I often tried to argue that I could still live in Israel working for reconciliation and not participating in violence. But he argued that it wasn't our individual deeds or misdeeds that upset the Palestinians, it was the system, the very existence of the nation of Israel that displaced them.

More and more, I began to feel that the problem was not a national one. It somehow touched on the whole destiny of humanity. I began to consider the history of the Jewish nation throughout the centuries. On the one hand, Israel was a nation like other nations, made up of human beings like other human beings. Again and again, the people had sought to establish themselves by strength and might. But the Jewish people had always been aware of another task: to live out an example of righteousness and justice among the nations. There had always been prophetic voices calling the people back to this special task. I was still a convinced atheist, but something of this began to work in me.

Of course, Uncle Chaim Simcha was witness to all my grappling. As I began to feel more and more that I should leave Israel and seek a deeper answer to the need of mankind, he tried to dissuade me. He said that the needs of people are the same everywhere; I did not need to go on a long quest. But I was restless and I felt I needed to leave Israel to find clarity. Finally, he said rather sadly, 'Here is another one in our family who is seeking the Messiah.' Maybe he was referring to his own youthful idealism or maybe he was referring to my cousin Leibich. In the 1920's he had gone to Palestine, but he was expelled when he became a communist. He came back to Poland, but eventually went to fight in the Spanish Civil War and never returned. Maybe there was a special strain of seekers and dreamers in our family; or maybe it is in the nature of the Jewish people. I do not believe it is just coincidence that so many Jews have committed themselves to different freedom and justice movements around the world.

In any case, I began to prepare to leave Israel. I wanted to go to Paris. After the war, Paris was a meeting-place for many nationalities and ideologies. I hoped to get work as a lino-typist in Yiddish, so I spent six months training for that trade. Meanwhile, I worked night and day to learn French. Finally, I left Israel for Paris in May 1953.

14. The Paris Group

My MAIN CONTACT IN PARIS was my cousin Berta who had moved there from Israel a year earlier. Through Berta, I met Jakob Halperin, whom she later married. Jakob was a gifted speaker and he headed up a committed group of Leninists in Paris. Looking back, I can see now that Berta and some of her friends in Tel Aviv had spotted me long before as a possible recruit for their Leninist group. Before she left, we had talked about the things that concerned me and about my idea of leaving Israel. But at the time, I didn't have any idea that she was involved in such things. I assumed she was being nice to me just because she was my cousin and we shared some similar ideas. But by the time I arrived in Paris, I was much more open to their communist ideals.

Jakob could win over almost anyone. He knew Russian, Polish, Arabic, Hebrew, German and other languages perfectly. He was well read and had an in-depth knowledge of classical literature. Lenin was his model. He criticized Trotsky, Stalin and other communist leaders for betraying

Lenin's vision. He was a convinced idealist and dedicated his whole life for the communist revolution. In fact, he was prepared to use almost any means to achieve his goal of a just society.

I was involved for about three months in this paradoxical community. We had lots of comradeship, ate together, and basically shared everything. But the circle was quite guarded. We met for secret discussion groups, but we didn't tell each other our names or anything about our backgrounds. They produced some leaflets to further the cause of 'true communism', but these were directed more against Stalin than against the capitalists. They said 'Yes, we are a small group, but in Russia they were also only a few people and that movement grew. We have to be ahead of the masses and then they will follow.'

After about three months, I moved on to live with my brother and sister in Frankfurt. I would have stayed longer with the group in Paris, but I couldn't get permission to remain in France. During this time, my sister Judith managed to come from Israel for her first visit, so we four siblings finally met again after our scattered odyssey through Europe and Asia. I must have been in Germany for six months or so, but I didn't find work there and I still longed to return to my comrades in Paris.

Early in 1954, my friends help me slip back into France. By devious means I first crossed the border into Belgium and then got into France. Everything worked out well, but ironically my troubles started after I reached Paris. No one met me at the station as planned, and I didn't have anywhere to go for the night. I didn't want to arouse questions or suspicions by hanging around the station, so I wandered to a part of Paris which had plenty of nightlife. By then, it was quite late, so I settled onto a bench to wait for morning.

After a time, a man came along and struck up a conversation. This man was also a foreigner and told stories of how he had been mistreated. My sympathy grew into utter stupidity. I told him that I was there illegally. He asked me if I had enough money to get by on and I assured him that I did, even showing him my purse. Shortly afterwards, he wished me all the best and wandered off. Later, I went to buy a cup of coffee and found that all my money had been stolen.

I survived, though, and the next day I found Jakob and Berta who helped me find a place to live. In France, you have to register your address with the authorities, so that was a problem. I moved around to different places, but finally a member of our group helped me find something a little more permanent. He was a student and lived in a house where the *concierge*, or housemistress, sat by the door and watched everyone going in or out. He told her he was going back to Corsica for a time and would like for me to use his room. Each day I went in and out, careful never to say anything more than '*Bonjour, Madame!*', so that she couldn't recognize that I wasn't an ordinary French student. It was only really difficult when I had to pay the rent. I had to learn my lines very exactly for such occasions.

In our group, we studied Marx and Lenin. We had

discussions and even went on retreats together. I longed for a society where people can live together in harmony with no injustice and no poor. So some of their Marxist theories seemed to provide hope for a solution: for example, the idea that society determines people's behaviour. It is quite obvious that someone who grows up in the slums behaves differently from people who grow up in a different environment. So it seems an obvious conclusion that if we change the circumstances of people's lives, then they will also act differently. The capitalist system encourages egotism because of the way each one fends for oneself. A socialist system should therefore encourage sharing and community.

But there were also some questions where I couldn't find a satisfactory answer within that group. I didn't want to see the developments in Russia repeat themselves. How could I be sure that future revolutions would not lead to the same tyranny and injustice I had seen in the Soviet Union?

Even in the French Revolution, the cry had been 'fraternity, liberty and equality', but those who seized power went on to commit terrible atrocities. The ideas were good, but was violent revolution really the way to realize those ideas?

I was also unhappy that hatred was represented as a necessity by the group. I could understand that a revolutionary has to identify with the masses and be willing to fight for them, but that was not the same to me as hatred against people. I discussed this issue many times with Berta, but she always asked, 'What about Hitler?' She had just managed to escape the Nazis as a 16-year old and she had tremendous hatred of Hitler and his government. I could only answer that I would be ready to kill tyrants and ready to fight for the revolution, but that it is wrong to hate anyone – even Hitler. Hatred is beneath human dignity; it degrades a human being into an animal. She would only respond, 'Josef, you are just like a Christian, a *petit bourgeois.*'

After about three months of this, I felt that I had to move on. I did not break with this group, but I had not yet found what I was looking for. I went to Germany. My brother and sister wanted me to join their business, but I wasn't interested. I found construction work in Frankfurt – hard physical work, hauling and digging. I had a tough time. There was no one who understood my longing. The unresolved tension was more than I could bear. I occasionally went to a psychoanalyst and sometimes I turned to alcohol. That was a dark time for me.

Jakob Halperin came over during this time and I travelled around with him as he tried to contact different socialist groups who opposed Stalinism but still worked for revolution. But my heart did not respond to what they were seeking. A communist society appealed to me, but I had doubts about Marx and I knew what had happened in Russia. I wanted to understand why it always goes wrong. People have made efforts to do it and there is a longing in people, but something prevents true community. For the time being, I tried to find joy earning my living by hard work, but I was still seeking something that I couldn't find.

I was pretty lonely.

By 1956, I felt I should make a new try in Israel. I was not prepared to participate in war or violence, but I thought I could try living in a kibbutz. I arrived just as the Suez Crisis broke out. Together with the British and French, Israel had taken over the Suez Canal and managed to conquer the whole Sinai Peninsula. There was a terrific euphoria in Israel. It was like the Biblical times of King David when they had a whole empire. For me it had just the opposite effect; I was sad.

I went around the country but I was more and more depressed. I was about to join a kibbutz; I even had an interview. But I was still too restless, too hopeless. More out of despair than conviction, I left Israel again to return to Germany. On the way, I stopped over in Rome. I was interested in seeing what attracted so many tourists there. I even went to the Vatican, although I was not at all interested in Catholicism or Christianity. While I was there, they suddenly closed the door behind us, and lo and behold, they carried the Pope in on a litter. He held his hands up, and all these people got into hysteria, just to see the Pope. This depressed me. I felt this was also against human dignity to lift up a person in such a way.

When I arrived in Germany in early 1957, I went to Munich instead of to Frankfurt. I'm not sure why. I was severely depressed – even suicidal at times. It could not go on and on that people hate and fight one another. If there was no solidarity among people, then there was no hope for the future, no purpose in living.

Things came to a real head when I went out drinking one night and someone stole all my money. I was now destitute on top of everything else. I even wrote a suicide note to Sammy trying to explain why I couldn't face living anymore. But a psychiatrist somehow encouraged me to give it more time; she even gave me some money to get by on. Somehow she managed to re-kindle something inside me. I began to gain more hope after I found a job and started working again.

In spite of my depression, I still hadn't given up my search. I went to courses and watched documentaries about the Hitler era. I wanted to understand how the Third Reich could have happened. When the neo-Nazi party held a rally in Munich I went to experience what kind of atmosphere was there. There may have been 1000 people sitting at tables in a beautiful hall. Waitresses with big muscles wandered around serving out huge steins of beer. A band played patriotic, rousing military music and emotions ran high. Then a man rose to speak. 'Do you see what they have done in Dresden? Do you hear the lies people tell about the German people? Do you see how our great German culture and heritage is despised by lying hypocrites?' I can't remember his words exactly, but he roused the people in that hall. I looked around and saw the many unemployed, hopeless people there and I could see how it happens. This man gave them hope, gave them a sense of belonging. Given the right circumstances, almost anyone could be sucked into such a 'community'.

Outing from Sinntal Bruderhof, August 1960

15. Breakthrough

AMONG THE COURSES I TOOK in Munich to fill my time was a course to learn Esperanto. I read various Esperanto newspapers and found out about various groups concerned about peace and justice. In one of the Esperanto newspapers, I read an advert from a man wanting to correspond with anyone interested in living a life based on giving what you can and receiving what you need. I responded and got in touch with a man in England named Derrick Faux. He told me about the Bruderhof communities and told me there was a Bruderhof in Germany, so I decided to visit in July 1958.

I was still grappling constantly with the question why people cannot live in community and solidarity. Why does it go wrong even when people want to live in community? I was sceptical. The religious side of the Bruderhof put me off. I was also not interested in an island of brotherhood in a sea of injustice and hate where people try to find some kind of personal peace and fulfilment. I wanted an answer for all mankind. At the same time I was in great personal need, because I hadn't found what I was seeking after years and years. So I thought, maybe I can learn something from a group of people trying to live together. Maybe I can understand why the ideals of justice and equality have not been realized in the various revolutions.

I was already apprehensive, thinking of the religious and Christian side of it, but I wanted to see them as human beings. I said to myself, 'Please, don't be prejudiced, and don't straight away judge people. Be open when you come.'

My resolve was put to the test from the first encounter. I arrived on a Sunday afternoon and the first person I met was a man walking up and down in front of the house balancing a stick on his head. I asked if this was the Bruderhof, and he confirmed it was without once taking his eyes off the stick. He just kept walking up and down, up and down. It seemed like there were some strange people here, or maybe they were not quite right in the head. But he did call someone over to take me in for a cup of tea.

Afterwards, there was a circus for the children. The man outside had been practicing his routine. That explained his unusual behaviour, but the whole episode was still quite strange. I was concerned about the destiny of mankind, and here no one seemed concerned about anything more serious than a children's circus.

After the circus, people approached me and asked what I was looking for, why I had come. In the end, I stayed for a couple of weeks. On the last day of my visit, they asked me to tell at a mealtime what the visit had meant to me. I said again what I always said, 'I am seeking brotherhood. I am seeking an answer to the need of mankind. I long for this, I am ready to give my life for it.' I couldn't agree with these people's ideas, but they took an interest in what I was seeking and they were obviously seeking something themselves.

I went back to Munich, but I was eager to go back to the Bruderhof – still trying to find out what it is that prevents people living together in peace. In my letter requesting to come back, I wrote: 'I long to once experience in my life, in my heart, the answer to the deepest need of mankind. Even if I can experience the answer for only one minute, that will be enough for me.' I never want to forget that sentence, because that was my longing at the time and I have since experienced so much more than that.

I came for a second visit in September 1958. The members of the community welcomed me warmly into their circle. We lived very simply: there was practically no heating and food was scarce. For breakfast we had a tiny piece of cheese and some bread to divide among ourselves. The man responsible for buying food even asked me if I could lend them some money. I gave him everything I had.

I came to love those people and I wanted to stay longer. But I was very outspoken about what I felt. I respected that they were Christians and had their beliefs – I could never have made light of other people's beliefs – but I wondered why we couldn't live for justice without having a faith in God. I also felt that it would be mockery or hypocrisy if I joined in any religious activity. Whenever they sang a song with religious meaning, I simply remained quiet. This was not always easy for me, because they sang often – especially as Christmas approached – but I was principled. I also refused to take part in the Christmas play for the same reason. But if a song was non-religious, I joined in with gusto. I am actually surprised that they let me stay. We were a small group with many guests and it must have taxed everyone's patience that I was constantly questioning the religious basis of the community.

And indeed, shortly after New Year, someone came to me and said, 'Josef, why do you have to argue so much about the different aspects of our community life, ideology, and belief? Are you looking for brotherhood? If so, come and live it out with us. Don't just talk about it.' They wanted me to take an active part instead of just standing by as an observer and critic. This made sense to me and I said I would do it. I could experiment by living it out myself. But what I then experienced came as quite a shock.

Through my whole Marxist outlook, I was convinced that outward circumstances determine people's behaviour. I assumed that the ideal society would ensure ideal brotherhood. Of course, I had already begun to have doubts, because all efforts so far to create this ideal society had failed utterly. But when I actually tried living in community, I saw that there was something inside myself that opposed it. Even under seemingly ideal circumstances, something stands in the way of true brotherhood, true solidarity: ego, self-will and touchiness were not a result of some outward influence; they were at the heart of my very being. This was a shock. Was my search in vain? What should I do now? I was at a crossroads.

At the peak of my inner turmoil, a man named Heinrich Arnold visited from one of the Bruderhof communities in America. He had experienced many years of communal life and he was eager to talk to me. I shared with him my seeking and what I longed for. He just listened with great understanding and compassion; there were even tears in his eyes. Later, he wrote to me from America: 'Josef, I trust and believe that one day we will be brothers in community.' I wondered how he could think like this since inwardly I was still so far from accepting the basis of the Bruderhof life. I was still very much an atheist; I was not ready to accept any form of religious belief that I could not prove logically.

Whitsun 1959 proved to be the turning point. Many people, mostly students, came to a weekend conference at the Bruderhof. Heinz von Homeyer, the well-known author of *The Radiant Mountain*, was the keynote speaker. Of course, Whitsun was a religious festival and I had my ideas about that. So I was once again more an observer than a participant. One evening, a heated discussion raged between two opposing camps until it seemed that they had reached an impasse. I don't remember exactly what the issue was, but by the end they were just shouting at one another. Then a man stood up and said, 'Dear people, I want to say something. There are two spiritual powers in this world. There is a spiritual power that brings people together and there is a spiritual power that tears people apart. Which power do you want to listen to in your heart?' Then he sat down. Quite suddenly there was a change in the atmosphere in that room. People were able to communicate with one another and there was quite a sharing. The walls that had stood between people only moments before had vanished.

Something was happening in that room that I could not fathom. Then it struck me. I can't say why it happened at that moment, but something struck my heart. In that moment, I felt the reality of the power of Christ who through the centuries has wanted to gather a people into unity, into brotherhood. It was this same vision that the Jewish nation was called to represent, to be an example of a completely new way of life in this world. At that moment this power completely overwhelmed me and changed my life.

This was the complete opposite of the caricature of Christianity that I had seen in the pogroms of Poland, the frenzied masses in Rome, the self-satisfied Christians in so many places who seek only their own salvation and who persecuted my people. It was not a sweet, personal religious experience; I had found the answer to the deep, burning need of mankind – the key to the true peace and justice that all people long for. Until that moment, my inexorable logic had excluded any such spiritual dimension. But from that point on, I have had no doubt. I found what I had been seeking. This is the only answer to mankind's need, to open themselves to the spirit of God who wants to gather a people to live out his will.

I love the game of chess. In chess, it often takes a long time before you make a move. You look at all the possibilities and then you decide on your move. It looks completely logical since everything is all thought through. But sometimes your opponent makes a move that you hadn't thought of at all; it goes against your whole logic. You realize that your whole approach was built on a false premise. You have to start from scratch, as if it were a completely new game.

'I long to once experience in my life, in my heart, the answer to the deepest need of mankind. Even if I can experience the answer for only one minute, that will be enough for me.' Yes, I have experienced that it is possible for men, women, and children, for Jews, Arabs, Germans, Africans, Americans, and Asians to live together in peace and brotherhood. It is possible to overcome the forces of evil that tear people apart. I still want to give my life for this longing and for its fulfilment.

Postscript

"O PEOPLE OF JACOB, come let us walk in the light of the Lord." (Is. 2:5) Let us follow the divine light with all our strength, in trembling, but resolutely. Perhaps in so doing we will be an example, a sign for others, an escape from darkness towards the light. Let us reject the empty boasting to ourselves and others of being the chosen people. Let us show our chosenness through the deeds of daily life, putting into practice what our heavenly Father has called us to be; an example and a splendour to all the nations, to all people.

Natan Hofshi

AS A MEMBER OF THE BRUDERHOF, Josef threw himself into this new life, to put into practice the answers that he found. But news of the continuing conflict in Israel continued to trouble him, along with the painful memories of his own role in the earlier years of that conflict. He could still see in his mind's eye the faces of the people of Lod whom his unit drove from their homes, and further back his own memories of being driven from his home in Poland.

Then in 1997, almost fifty years after those events in Lod, he came into contact with an Israeli Arab living in Lod, Jakoub Munayeer. After a brief correspondence, he travelled to Lod and met with Jakoub. Josef was able to ask Jakoub's forgiveness for what happened and to feel his outreaching love. They spent time recounting to each other their experiences of those troubled days in 1948 and found complete personal reconciliation. In a way it was a small step, just one story against the daily flood of suicide bombs and revenge attacks. But as Josef says: "Maybe it will start a chain reaction. Violence calls for violence, but by starting another process, by reaching out a hand, finding forgiveness and reconciliation, this could spread. Each of us can do this in our interpersonal relationships, to ask for forgiveness and try to build a better world".

Josef and his wife Ruth have seven children: Channah, Shulamite, Chaim, Eldad, Tikva, Ephraim and Mina. They live at the Darvell Bruderhof in England. Josef is actively involved in promoting forgiveness and reconciliation between people. Most of all, he works to keep the vision alive that there is another way, that men and women can live together in peace.